Affirmations for Kids: Improving Self-Motivation, Self-Confidence and Self-Esteem

By
Paige Moss

Other Books by Paige Moss

I Help Around The House: Picture Book About Being Responsible & Making Chores Fun

I am Happy & Thankful Because...: Expressing Gratitude at Home (Picture Book)

More Books by Paige Moss
amazon.com/author/paigemoss

Dedication

To my daughters and granddaughters who truly inspire me.

I love you.

Paige Moss

Your monster friends are here.

We want to share with you some of our favorite affirmations.

We hope that you find some that you like and maybe create your own.

#1
Today is going to be a great day.

#2
Amazing and awesome things happen to me.

#3
I am loved by my family.

#4
They love me for who I am.

#5
My friends love and respect me.

#6
I make friends easily.

#7
I deserve all good things.

#8
I have a wonderful imagination.

#9
I believe in myself.

#10
I can do anything I set my mind to do.

#11
I learn from my mistakes and challenges.

#12
I do my best to help at home.

#13
I am excited about the future.

#14
Every day is a new adventure.

#15
I am open to learn new things.

#16
Learning is fun and exciting.

#17
I am strong and confident.

#18
I am patient.

#19
I am respectful of others.

#20

With practice and patience, I get better and better every day.

#21
I forgive others for their mistakes.
No one is perfect.

#22

I forgive myself for my mistakes.
I learn from my mistakes.

#23
All of my problems have solutions.

#24
I stand up for what I believe in.

#25
My happiness is up to me and no one else.

#26
I am a fast learner.

#27
I face my fears and overcome them.

#28
I have an attitude of gratitude.

#29
I am confident in my abilities.

#30
I am honest and trustworthy.

#31
I am in control of my emotions.

#32
I do my very best in school.

#33
I am special, in my own way.

Dear reader:

I hope you enjoyed reading this book. There are a series of books created to assist children in their daily lives. These books were created to help children stay motivated, have fun and, most of all, remain balanced in this world of ups and downs.

To read more books from me, please visit my Amazon Author page at:
amazon.com/author/paigemoss

Also, please write a review for this book. It is greatly appreciated.

www.ingramcontent.com/pod-product-compliance
Lightning Source LLC
Chambersburg PA
CBHW042126030726
47599CB00002B/363